Marketing Management Concepts and Tools:

A Simple Introduction

Also by K.H. Erickson

<u>Simple Introductions</u>

Accounting and Finance Formulas
Choice Theory
Corporate Finance Formulas
Econometrics
Financial Economics
Game Theory
Game Theory for Business
Investment Appraisal
Marketing Management Concepts and Tools
Mathematical Formulas for Economics and Business
Microeconomics

Marketing Management Concepts and Tools:

A Simple Introduction

K.H. Erickson

© 2014 K.H. Erickson

All rights reserved.

No part of this publication may be reproduced, stored in or introduced into a retrieval system, or transmitted in any form or by any means, including electronic, mechanical, photocopying, recording or otherwise, without the prior permission of the author.

Contents

Marketing Essentials

Marketing defined

Marketing may be seen both as a set of doing tools or skill and as a holistic concept, and is popularly defined as:

'Selling goods which don't come back to people who do'

From sellers' markets to buyers' markets

Recent years have seen a *shift from sellers' markets to buyers' markets*, with businesses forced to respond to a new marketing environment:

1. Value is now greatly influenced by buyers
2. Value is now quality relative to cost price
3. Value now defined as market-perceived value (MPV)

The 7 Ps of marketing

The original 4 Ps of marketing are:

Product, Price, Place, Promotion

But three changes to the marketing environment have added another 3 Ps:

People, Process, Physical evidence

The 6 Cs of marketing

In a new marketing environment many prefer 6 Cs:

Context, Customer, Competition, Cash/Cost, Channels, Company

Management Objectives and Tasks

Company goals

Profitability, Shareholder value, Customer satisfaction, Growth

Stakeholders

Firms manage objectives and constraints of stakeholders:

Shareholders, Managers, Customers, Employers, Creditors

Balancing objectives

The diverse objectives of stakeholders are managed with:

1. Balanced organizational representation
2. Clear definition of the organization's mission
3. Creation of the 'balanced scorecard' to implement strategy and measure business performance

Strategy development

Strategy offers *focus, cost leadership, and differentiation* and is based on two main areas:

Resource allocation
Market penetration, Product development, Diversification, Market development

Building a sustainable competitive advantage
Develop market perceived value (MPV), Build a brand, Create legal entry barriers, Use learning curve advantage

Strategic intentions and success factors

Fitting to market environment, Speed and decisiveness, Timing, Balancing efficiency and effectiveness, Organizational effectiveness

Core company competencies

Discovery of what customers value
Use of skills to create the right value offerings

5 organizational dimensions

People, Structure, Strategy, Systems, Leadership

A Customer-Led Business

Marketing theory

Marketing is based on several linked ideas, which all relate back to a marketing environment *led by customers* where companies seek out a best response to them:

Needs & products, Value & choice, Exchange & markets, Markets & capitalism

5 tasks of marketing management

1. Identification of target markets
2. Marketing research
3. Product development
4. Creation of a marketing mix
5. Monitor marketing

Operating philosophies

Product orientation
Sales orientation
Financial orientation
Customer orientation

Business success

With a customer-led business world the success of a single business will depend upon its ability to:

Achieve customer satisfaction, Gain customer loyalty

Focusing on market needs

With MPV defining value markets must be identified:

Existing markets, Latent markets (undeveloped or hidden), Incipient markets (developing)

A well-functioning organization

'Moments of truth' are where contact or an interaction between customer and business give the customer an opportunity to form or change their impression of the firm

'A right-side up organization' is one which emphasizes customer service, with employees on the top and managers on the bottom focused on meeting their needs

'One for all and all for one' describes the place of marketing relative to the business as a whole, and marketing is a central dimension of the entire business

Competitive advantage

To stay ahead of competitors and meet customer needs more effectively requires competitive benchmarking:

1. Determine the critical success factors (CSFs)
2. Discover customer's perceptions of the CSFs
3. Find how customers rate business competitors
4. Assess the gap between performance and MPV
5. Create action plans

Bain customer retention model

The Bain model sees customers as assets to be retained:

Cost of acquiring new customers may be high
Loyal customers often spend more
Costs less to serve customers who place regular orders
Satisfied customers are the best form of promotion
Satisfied customers will pay premium prices
Retaining customers limits market entry for rivals

Creating a customer-led business

In practice most businesses aren't truly customer-led due to several factors:

The background of firms' top executives
A misunderstanding of how marketing works
A lack of commitment to customer satisfaction
Resistance to change and the idea of a buyers' market

To become a customer focused firm managers and employees must buy into a vision of what they'd like the firm to be, and there are six overall steps in the process to change into a customer-led business:

1. Mission
2. Marketing audit
3. Strategy formation
4. Education and training
5. Implementation
6. Maintenance

Segmentation, Targeting and Positioning

Segmentation definition and requirements

Segmentation is the *'identification of individuals or organizations with similar market perceived value (MPV), to create groups to serve more effectively and which are of a sufficient size to be supplied efficiently'*, and it requires:

Segments are suitable, Hold sufficient viable potential, Segments are measureable

Benefits of segmentation

Target market selection, Tailored marketing mix, Differentiation, Opportunities and threats addressed

Consumer segmentation

Behavioural factors
Benefits sought, Purchase occasion, Purchase behaviour, Perceptions and benefits, Usage

Psychographic factors
Lifestyle, Personality

Profile factors
Demographic, Socioeconomic, Geographic

Business to business (B2B) segmentation

This segments businesses into their organizational markets at the macro level, and then again at the micro level:

Macro segmentation
Organization size, Industry, Geographic location

Micro segmentation
Choice criterion: Reliability, Convenience, and Price
Decision making structure and process
Purchasing organization

Targeting strategies

1. Undifferentiated marketing
2. Differentiated marketing: a distinct value offering (VO)
for each segment
3. Focused marketing: targeting a single segment
4. Customized marketing: a distinct value offering for key
customers

Positioning

Positioning involves two steps:

1. Targeted consumer segments receive the right value offering
2. Favourable connotations placed in minds of consumers to create a successful brand

Strategic Market Planning

Strategic windows

Major causes of strategic window openings which facilitate an adaption to change include:

New technology, New segment, New distribution channel, New legislation, Redefined markets, Environmental shock

Lagged responses to environmental change

Firms may have slow and delayed responses to market events due to:

Observation delays, Procrastination delays, Retrenchment, Power shifts

But lagged responses to change can be reduced with:

Effective management information systems
Enhancement of strategic capabilities
Corporate flexibility
Rapid transfers of power

Hierarchy of planning strategies

Firms have a hierarchy of strategic plans, and from top to bottom they are:

Corporate strategy, Divisional, Individual business

Strategic planning components

Firm scope, Business objectives, Resource allocation, Strategic business unit (SBU) identification, Synergy, Development of sustainable competitive advantage, Effective functional strategies

Corporate strategy variations

Firms may be defined by their type of corporate strategy:

Strategic planning, Financial control, Strategic control

Corporate strategy steps

1. Corporate mission statement
Define corporate scope, Create strategic intent or vision, Assessment of competencies and competitive advantage, Determine key stakeholders

2. Corporate objectives
Market share, Innovation, Resources, Productivity, Social, Profit

3. Identify SBUs based on features
Customer group factor, Customer needs factor, Technology factor

4. Resource allocation
Resources can be allocated to the SBUs based on the Boston Consulting Group (BCG) growth-share matrix concept:

Stars = Market leader, High growth
Cash cows = High market share, Low growth
Question marks = Low market share, High growth
Dogs = Low market share, Low growth

5. Explore synergies
Efficiency gains may be possible

6. Corporate development
This involves both internal and external growth:
Internal growth: Market penetration, Market development, Product development
External growth: Industry structure analysis using Porter's five forces model

Porter's five forces model

The model points to five forces which affect an industry:

Supplier bargaining power, Customer bargaining power, Threat of new entrants, Threat of substitute products, Rivalry with competitors within an industry

Business unit strategy components

1. Business mission

2. Strategic focus
Personnel differentiation, Image differentiation and brand, Price value and market perceived value (MPV) analysis, Market offering differentiation and MPV

3. Competitive advantage

4. Strategic objectives

5. Customer targets

6. Marketing mix

7. Resource allocation

8. Competitor targets

Determine who competitors are, Discover their objectives, Discover competitors' strengths and weaknesses, Determine their likely strategies, Decide what to do

9. Implementation and control

The McKinsey 7 S framework can be used:

Strategy, Structure, Systems, Skills, Shared values, Style, Staff

Market Dynamics and Competitive Strategy

Product life cycle

A product is thought to go through four stages in its life:

Introduction: Slow increase in sales and no profit
Growth: Significant increase in sales and good profits
Maturity: Sales and profits slow and stagnate
Decline: Sales decline and profits disappear

However, there are weaknesses to this concept:

No common life cycle pattern and stages may be repeated
Turning points between stages are unpredictable
Model is not exogenous and ignores external influences
Concept is product orientated only

Market dynamics

Market dynamics may be divided into two strategies, with the dynamics affected by competitors or customers respectively:

Competitor influence
New entrants, Supplier competition, Substitute technology

Customer influence
New users, New wants, Increasing firm knowledge

Evolutionary forces and 4 phases

This is similar to the product life cycle but examines the market as a whole:

Emerging market, High-growth, Mature phase, Decline

In the decline phase a firm has several strategic options:

Leadership, Niche, Harvest, Divest

Marketing strategy formulation

Strategies for a market pioneer
Demonstrate a differential advantage, Higher prices, Create switching costs, Economies of scale and experience

Strategies for defending market share
Position defence, Flanking defence, Pre-emptive defence, Counter-offensive, Mobile defence, Contraction defence

Strategies for a market challenger
Effective early strategies include:
Seek new markets, Seek new product attributes

Kotler and Singh give 5 attacking strategies:

Frontal attack, Flanking attack, Encirclement attack, Guerrilla attack, Bypass attack

Niche companies

In the early and growth stages of the market viable niche strategies include:

Separate niche, Separate cost structure, Cyclical stability, Exploit a lack of strategic interest in market from rivals, Limited potential in the market for competitors

Building a Successful Brand

Products and brands

A successful brand is a value package:

Product + Brand = Successful brand

Added values

Added values occur with:

Experience of use, User associations, Efficacy belief, Brand appearance, Name of manufacturer

A positioning strategy can achieve this with:

Attribute research, Competitor research, Gap analysis, Concept testing

Brand analysis can reveal if the positioning strategy is working as planned, and the analysis examines the characteristics of the brand:

'Brand essence' is the enduring soul of the brand, and the single idea which links its emotional and functional roles

'Brand personality' is the brand image in terms of human characteristics

'Values of users' are what brand users care about most

'Emotional rewards' are the expected emotional benefits from brand use

'Functional benefits' are the expected tangible benefits from brand use

'Attributes' are the tangible features of the product

Building brands

1. Tangible product

2. Basic brand
This builds on a tangible product with:
Brand name, Pack, Features, Quality, Design

3. Augmented brand
This stage is about making the brand a reality:
Delivery and installation, Service, Credit and terms of use, Guarantees

4. Potential brand
With all the previous brand building stages complete the brand has the potential to be a success

5. Process of brand growth

The potential brand becomes a success with active efforts from the company:

Advertising, Presentations, Display, Selling, Promotion, Public relations (PR)

And with customer behaviour which reinforces itself:

Trial, Differentiation, Satisfied customers, Added values, Loyalty, Brand equity

A successful brand increases a firm's market share and profits, generating the resources to create additional brands

Multibranding, line and brand extensions

A firm has several methods to build a brand:

Line extensions, Multibrands (e.g. Proctor and Gamble), Brand extensions (e.g. Virgin), Horizontal branding, Vertical branding

Improving brand performance

A firm can improve the performance of its brand by targeting one of two goals:

Increased volume of sales
Brand revitalization, Brand repositioning

Increased productivity
Brand revitalization, Brand elimination, Increased prices, Reduced costs

Buying a brand

Instead of creating a brand of its own a firm may find it easier to buy a ready-made brand from another company, but a bought brand may fail for several reasons:

Excessive debt levels, Disconnected brand portfolios, Inadequate skills, Firm overpaid for brand

Brand valuation can be based on a number of methods:

Price premium valuation, Incremental sales valuation, Replacement cost valuation, Stock market valuation, Future earnings valuation

Brand name importance

Brand name can embody MPV, Create a brand mnemonic, Ensure the brand makes a difference (MAD)

Poor brand management

The brand a firm creates may fail if brand management is poor, and common causes include:

Brand management by numbers not according to MPV, Excessive prices, Low investment

Consumer Behaviour

Human behaviour

<u>Consumer roles</u>
Users, Payers, Buyers

<u>Consumer desires</u>
Needs, Wants, Demands

Consumer perception

Perception is a process where an individual interacts with the environment and it contains three stages:

1. Sensing
2. Organizing
3. Interpreting

Perception is affected by:

Stimulus features, Contexts, Consumer characteristics

Consumer learning

Learning can be described as a change in the long-term memory, and there are four different learning mechanisms:

Cognitive learning, Modelling, Classical conditioning, Instrumental conditioning

Consumer motivation

Motivation is what gets people to act, and there are various different motivations:

1. Maslow's hierarchy of needs (from bottom to top)
Physiological needs
Safety and security needs
Love and belonging needs
Self-esteem needs
Self-actualization needs

2. Consumer emotions

3. Consumer mood factors
Advertising tone and manner, Salesperson demeanour, Value offering's sensory features, Store ambience

4. Involvement

5. Psychographics
Values, Self-conception, Lifestyle, Attitudes

Individual consumer decision making

The process proceeds as follows:

1. Problem recognition
2. Information search
3. Alternative evaluation
4. Purchase
5. Post-purchase evaluations

Household decision making

Family decision making steps decided by parents:

1. Beginning of buying decision process
2. Gathering and sharing of information
3. Evaluation and decision
4. Shopping and purchase
5. Conflict management

But these planned steps can be ruined by children due to:

Pester power

Market Research

Market research defined

Market research is *'the collection and analysis of opinion or characteristic data from individuals or organizations, and includes all forms of marketing and social research such as surveys and studies'*

The purpose of marketing research is to *'gain information about customers' needs and wants, to determine marketing opportunities for particular market offerings or value packages, to note changes in tastes or buying trends, and to assess the threats and insights offered by competitors'*

Research issues

The starting point in research is with two questions:

What is the problem to be researched?
What is the cause of the problem?

The 5Ws and H technique can be used for research issues:

Who? What? Where? When? Why? How?

Research methods

There are three types of research:

Exploratory, Descriptive, Causal

There are two main concerns when conducting research:

Reliability: Can the same results be repeated?
Validity: Has the research measured what it should have?

Data collection

Primary
Observation = Personal, Mechanical
Surveys = Mail, E-mail, Internet, Interviews, Telephone

Secondary
Internal sources = Accounting records
External sources = Periodicals, Government publications, Census, The World Wide Web

Recording research

Research results should be presented to managers in an easily understood form, and a typical report format is:

1. Background

2. Sample

3. Data collection

4. Results presentation

Ethical concerns when undertaking research

'Sugging' is a process where a firm tries to sell its products under the guise of conducting research, and this dishonest method of selling can challenge the legitimacy of undertaking research

Business to Business (B2B) Marketing

Business market customers

Customer types in a business market are:

Commercial customers
Concentration of customers, Significant purchasing power

Government customers
Negotiated contract

Institutional customers

Business market characteristics

Demand in a business market may exhibit various trends:

Derived demand: depends on demand for other products
Fluctuating demand: demand is up and down
Stimulated demand: demand must be generated by firms

B2B marketing is also known for close buyer-seller relationships with:

Supply chain management (just in time production), Relationship marketing

Organizational buying process

The major stages of the organizational buying process are:

1. Problem recognition
2. General need description
3. Product specifications
4. Search for supplier
5. Acquisition and proposals analysis
6. Selection of supplier
7. Delivery arrangement selection
8. Performance review

Major buying situations include:

New tasks, Straight rebuy, Modified rebuy

Major influences on organizational buyers are:

Market environment forces, Organizational forces, Individual forces, Group forces for buying participants

Innovation and New Product Development

Innovation defined

Innovation is the *'development and delivery of value packages to offer new and superior market perceived value for customers'*

To deliver innovation a new product must be:

Important, Unique, Sustainable, Marketable

Types of innovation include:

Product improvement, Cost reduction, Repositioning, Product line extension, Penetration of new market, Introduction of new product line

Reasons to innovate

There are two main reasons to seek innovation:

To secure niche position, Lower costs

Strategic benefits with fast innovation

New market creation, Expansion of current markets, Increased market penetration, Business repositioning, Market share defence

Barriers to innovation

External barriers to innovation include:

Shortening product life cycles, Additional new products, Global competition, Increasingly segmented markets, Increasing environment and consumer legislation, Increasing costs linked with development of new products, Declining profitability of brand followers

Internal mismanagement causes of innovation failure are:

Excessively slow development, No differential advantage, Unenthusiastic management, Poor planning

Preparing for innovation

Keeping the following areas in order supports innovation:

Vision and objectives, People and skills, Customer focus, Autonomous teams, Systems and integration

Product development process

1. Corporate strategy and innovation
2. New product ideas
3. Screening of ideas
4. Concept development
5. Business analysis and brand development
6. Implementation

Customer adoption process

The product adoption process for a new innovation is:

1. Awareness
2. Interest
3. Evaluation
4. Trial
5. Adoption

Customers adopt a new innovation at different rates over time:

1. Innovators (2.5%)
2. Early adopters (13.5%)
3. Early majority (34%)
4. Late majority (34%)
5. Laggards (16%)

Services Marketing Strategy

Service characteristics

Intangibility
Services are a deed
Difficult for a customer to evaluate before the purchase

Inseparability
Production and consumption are simultaneous
Service provider plays vital role
Good staff selection and training is important

Homogeneity
Service variability may be a problem
Staff selection and training vital to ensure homogeneity
Evaluations systems required
Reliable equipment needed

Perishability
Consumption can't be stored for future use
Supply must be matched with demand
Off-peak demand must be stimulated
Differential pricing necessary to change demand

Service management

The organizational benefits of offering good service include:

Increased purchases, Lifetime value of customers, Sustainable competitive advantages, Customer retention, Word of mouth recommendation value

The benefits the customer receives from good service are:

Higher quality service, Switching costs are avoided, Reduced levels of stress and risk

Internet Marketing

Types of internet marketing

Electronic commerce (e-commerce)
Electronic marketing (e-marketing)

The key benefit associated with internet marketing is the *ability of marketers and customers to share information, and facilitate customer relationship management* (CRM)

E-marketing characteristics

Addressability
Website visitors can be identified
Visitors can reveal data on their needs before purchase
Website visitors can be encouraged to register
Cookies can track visitor frequency for requirements

Interactivity
Customers can communicate details of their needs
Marketers can build on the idea of a community

Memory
Enables real-time formation, retrieval and use of data
Specialized software can be targeted to a customer

Control
Customer can control what they view
Customers can influence what is shown on websites

Accessibility
Information can be gathered, URLs can be personalized,
Increased supplier competition makes firms more creative

Digitalization
Products and attributes shown as digital information parts
Software allows buyers to track their orders
Digitalization facilitates faster customer value offerings

E-commerce market exchanges

From Business to Business (B2B), e.g. Cisco
From Business to Consumer (B2C), e.g. Amazon
From Consumer to Business (C2B), e.g. Priceline
From Consumer to Consumer (C2C), e.g. eBay

Factors affecting internet marketing adoption

Internal, Environmental, Comparative advantage

Benefits and limitations of e-commerce

Consumer e-commerce benefits
Convenience, An information resource, Multimedia, Reduced prices, New market process outsourcing

Limitation of e-commerce for consumers
Potentially slow delivery times, Information overload, Dependent on access to technology, Security issues, Potentially costly

Business e-commerce benefits
Lower investment, Lower order costs, Better distribution, Relationship building, Reduced selling, New opportunity, Customized promotion

Limitations of e-commerce for businesses
Costly set-up, Incurs operational costs, Short-termist, Costly content, Over-specialized, Technology dependent

Online marketing assessment

Online marketing can be assessed on the basis of:

Strategic competence, Financial competence, Innovation, Workforce, Quality, Productivity, Information Systems

Superior online marketing strategy

To excel in online marketing a business can aim to offer some or all of the following qualities:

Lower costs for lower prices, Better service quality, Customization of products, Greater product variety

Marketing Communications

The role of marketing communications

Marketing communications are designed to *'facilitate exchanges and transactions with individuals, groups, or organizations by informing and persuading them to buy a company's products'*. The process is known as *promotion*:

Promotion process

1. Source (company)
2. Coded message created
3. Message passes through medium
4. Decoded message formed
5. Audience receives decoded message

Promotion aims

Creation of category need, Increased brand awareness, Positive brand attitude, Create brand purchase intention, Purchase facilitation

Promotion tools

Publicity and public relations (PR), Sales promotion, Sponsorship, Direct mail, Advertising, Personal selling, Internet

Integrated marketing communications

Integrated marketing communication (IMC) is defined as *'Coordination and combination of all marketing communication tools, sources and channels within a company into an integrated system of promotion methods'*

Selection of promotional tools

The choice of promotional tools is decided by:

Product characteristics, Target market characteristics, Promotional resources, Promotional objectives, Promotional method cost and availability

Advertising

Advertising defined

Advertising is *'non-personal communication transmitted through mass media and which is paid for by the source company'*

An advertising campaign is *'advertising placed in various media in an attempt to reach a target market'*

Advertising goals

Promoting market process outsourcing (MPO) and firms
Stimulating primary demand (pioneer advertising)
Stimulating selective demand (competitive advertising)
Negate competitor advertising (comparative advertising)
Raise sales personnel effectiveness (defensive advertising)
Educating the market
Increasing the uses of an MPO
Reminding firm customers (reminder advertising)
Reducing sales fluctuations (reinforcement advertising)

Advertising campaign steps

First of all it needs to be decided who will be in charge of the advertising campaign, and it may be:

One or a few people in the firm, Advertising department, An external advertising agency

With a decision made on who develops the campaign a series of steps can then proceed:

1. Identify and conduct analysis on advertising target

2. Determine advertising objectives

3. Create an advertising platform with key selling points
Most important issues for consumers must be targeted, Research and surveys can reveal consumers' MPV, Combined internal and external analysis reveals key issues

4. Decide on advertising budget
There are a number of possible approaches in deciding an advertising budget:
Objective and task approach, Percentage of sales, Competition matching approach, Arbitrary approach

5. Develop media plan

The media plan decides which media to use for advertising and the dates and times it will appear, with key factors being:

Reach, Cost, Frequency

6. Creation of an advertising message

This involves the following:

Generation of AIDA (Attention, Interest, Desire Action), Copy, Modification for regional issues and differences, Storyboard/Artwork/Illustrations/Layout

7. Campaign execution

8. Evaluation of advertising effectiveness

Advertising effectiveness can be evaluated with:

Pre-tests, Consumer focus groups, Post-campaign tests, Spontaneous recall tests, Prompted recall tests, Recognition tests

Distribution Strategy

Channel intermediary functions

Distributors, or channel intermediaries, are used for several goals:

Reconcile producer and consumer needs (breaking bulk), Improving efficiency, Improving product accessibility, Providing specialist services

Distribution channels

Producer to Agent to Wholesaler to Retailer to Consumer
Producer to Wholesaler to Retailer to Consumer
Producer to Retailer to Consumer
Producer to Consumer

Industrial channels

Producer to Agent to Distributor to Consumer
Producer to Distributor to Business
Producer to Agent to Business
Producer to Business

Channel strategy

A channel strategy involves three separate parts:

Channel selection
Channel selection will be influenced by:
Market factors, Producer factors, Product factors, Competitive factors

Distribution intensity
Distribution intensity may be selected as:
Intensive distribution, Selective distribution, Exclusive

Channel integration
Channel integration may involve:
Conventional marketing channels, Channel ownership, Franchising

Channel management

Channel management includes several components to ensure all those people involved in the channels are on board with the project:

Channel selection, Motivation, Training, Evaluation, Managing conflict

Sources of channel conflict

Differences in goals, Differences in targeted product line, Performance issues, Multiple distribution channels

Ethical concerns

Distribution channels can create the potential for unethical practices:

'Slotting allowances' are fees charged by distributors to place a company's products on its shelves,
'Grey markets' are where a distribution channel trades through legal but unofficial and unauthorized markets,
'Exclusive dealing' is where a company is tied to a distribution channel and can't use others,
'Supply restrictions' are obstacles which will prevent some distribution channels from being used,
'Fair trading' is where anti-competitive practices are prevented

Pricing Strategy

Evaluating price competitiveness

This process determines how consumers perceive alternative price offers, and follows the steps:

1. Assessment of price competitiveness
2. Set price objectives
3. Strategic price focus
4. Targeting of market segment
5. Assess competitive strategies
6. Measure customer's market perceived value
7. Price product line
8. Choose price

Setting initial prices

Non-price factors affecting demand
Price won't solely be chosen based on expected demand as other factors also affect demand:
Supplier reputation for offering good service (value), Market communication effectiveness, Firm strategy, Market segmentation, High price can signal superiority

Firm objectives

And the firm's price will depend on its specific objectives: *Maintain market share, Harvest, Quality leadership, Growth*

Market evolution stage

The stage of the market will also play a role in the pricing decision:

Innovation stage = high prices

Mature stage = low prices

Decline stage = economy prices

Target market segments

Target market segments will have different prices:

Entry market, middle market, niche market

Competitor targets

Competitors will play a role in a firm's pricing:

Need to assess likely competitor reaction,

Level prices result in retaliatory pricing,

Market's major player has key role in firm's pricing

Customer value

Customer value also plays a role in price:

Market perceived value

Price offers to make a difference (MAD)

Product mix pricing

The pricing for products will also depend on the type of product:

Product lines, Follow-on products, Blocking products, Bundles products, Parallel imports

Making price changes

There are two approaches to changing product prices:

Cost reduction approach, Price increase approach

Other price factors

There are other factors which can affect the price of a firm's products and these include:

Cost-reducing innovation, Reseller mark-ups, Exit barriers

The Future of Marketing

Key trends

The key trends that will define the future of marketing are:

1. Relationship marketing
More profitable to retain customers than gain new ones,
But brand loyalty from consumers has never been lower,
Consumer switching costs are now lower than ever before,
B2B market growth is in value chains not supply chains

2. New technology
There are ongoing developments in information and communication technology with increasing influence of:
Telephone marketing, Email, Electronic brochures, Database marketing, Internet

3. Value transformation
Value defined by customers as market perceived value,
Customer satisfaction best indicator of long-run success,
Distinction between product and service is blurred,
Customer service increasingly important

4. Measurement and accountability

Measurement of consumer response to products is vital,
Measurement of long-run advertising results is important,
Brand equity and creation of known brand advantageous

5. Innovation and learning

New product development speed is an important factor,
First in industry (first move) vs second in (learn off rival),
Growing focus on new markets (expeditionary marketing)

6. Globalization

Marketing management now involves a global market,
Marketing must account for cultural differences globally,
Cost efficiency and knowledge sharing across borders

Firm responses to the future of marketing

Firms have four key tasks to manage the trends affecting the future of marketing:

1. Understand customers and prospects, with the use of marketing as a philosophy helpful in this end
2. Understand firm competitors
3. Understand how markets may change over time, with specialist marketing agencies useful
4. Understand the importance of strategy, and develop a strategic marketing perspective

www.ingramcontent.com/pod-product-compliance
Lightning Source LLC
Chambersburg PA
CBHW071815170526
45167CB00003B/1316